Weathervane, artist unknown,
late nineteenth century, painted
wood, New York State Historical
Association, Cooperstown

The Art of America in the Gilded Age

By Shirley Glubok

Designed by Gerard Nook

Macmillan Publishing Co., Inc.
New York
Collier Macmillan Publishers
London

The author gratefully acknowledges the kind assistance of:
Weston J. Naef, Assistant Curator, Department of Prints and Photographs, The Metropolitan Museum of Art;
Louis Sharp, Assistant Curator, American Paintings and Sculpture, The Metropolitan Museum of Art;
Natalie Spassky, Assistant Curator, American Paintings and Sculpture, The Metropolitan Museum of Art;
Roberta W. Wong, Prints Division, New York Public Library; *Joel Rosenbaum;*
and especially the helpful cooperation of *Stuart P. Feld* and *Marvin D. Schwartz.*

Front cover illustration: *The Hatch Family,* by Eastman Johnson, 1871, oil, The Metropolitan Museum of Art, Gift of Frederick H. Hatch, 1926. Back cover illustration: *The Open Air Breakfast,* by William Merritt Chase, about 1888, oil, The Toledo Museum of Art, Gift of Florence Scott Libbey, 1953.

Library of Congress Cataloging in Publication Data

Glubok, Shirley.   The art of America in the Gilded Age.   1. Art, American—History—Juvenile literature.
[1. Art, American—History]   I. Title.   N6510.G56   709'.73   73–6048   ISBN 0–02–736100–4

Bareback Riders, by W. H. Brown, 1886, oil on cardboard, National Gallery of Art, Collection of Edgar William and Bernice Chrysler Garbisch, 1958

When the Civil War ended in 1865, the American nation embarked on a period of enormous expansion and growth. New technologies were developing rapidly and new industries springing up.

As industry and commerce expanded, great private fortunes were made. The new millionaires built elaborate homes for themselves and collected works of art with which to fill them. Because of this lavish display of glittering wealth, the years after the Civil War until the closing days of the nineteenth century are sometimes called the "Gilded Age."

The Last of Old Westminster, 1862, oil, Museum of Fine Arts, Boston, Abraham Shuman Fund

As travel by railroad and steamship became easier, more American artists journeyed to Europe, especially to Paris, to study painting and sculpture. While most of them returned to America, others remained abroad. James Abbott McNeill Whistler lived most of his life in France and England. Among the many pictures he painted in London are a view of the new Westminster Bridge, as the scaffolding is being removed, and a portrait of Thomas Carlyle, a famous philosopher and writer. Painting a portrait in profile—viewed from the side—was unusual. The arrangement of the seated man, his hat, the chair and the pictures on the wall, forms an unexpected pattern of shapes, reflecting the painter's interest in Japanese art, which had become popular in Europe. The artist called this portrait *Arrangement in Grey and Black, Number 2*. Whistler's famous portrait of his mother, also painted in profile, was entitled *Arrangement in Grey and Black, Number 1*.

1872, oil,
Glasgow Art Gallery
and Museum

5

The Daughters of Edward D. Boit, 1882, oil, Museum of Fine Arts, Boston, Gift of Mary Louisa Boit,
Florence D. Boit, Jane Hubbard Boit, and Julia Overing Boit, in memory of their father

*J*ohn Singer Sargent was born in Italy of American parents who were living abroad. As a child he traveled widely through Europe, with his sketch pad always at hand. This street scene in Venice, where Sargent often visited, was painted with swift, flashing brush strokes. The flowing edges of the woman's skirt and shawl give her figure movement.

Although Sargent spent most of his life in London and Paris, he often went to America to do portraits of fashionable people. The four sisters at left were painted at home in Boston in an elegant room with huge Japanese vases and a Chinese rug. It was a symbol of high social position during the Gilded Age to have one's portrait painted by Sargent.

About 1891, oil, The Art
Institute of Chicago,
Robert A. Waller Fund

8

$\mathcal{M}$ary Cassatt was born in Pittsburgh but lived most of her life in Paris. In France she was the only American invited to exhibit her paintings with a group of French artists known as the "Impressionists," who experimented with the changing effects of light and atmosphere. Their aim was to show a moment in time, to paint what the eye would see at a glance. Viewing a scene from above and using bold outlines and strong patterns, as in *The Bath* at left, are ideas taken from Japanese prints.

While the country was entering a new era of industrialization, most American artists stayed in their private worlds, painting the people around them. Women friends and relatives were favorite subjects of Edmund C. Tarbell, who was a member of a group that became known as the "Ten American Painters." Most of The Ten studied in Paris and became interested in French Impressionist painting, then returned to practice and teach their art in America.

Mother and Child in Boat, 1892, oil, Museum of Fine Arts, Boston, Bequest of David P. Kimball in memory of his wife, Clara Bertram Kimball

In the Studio, about 1880, oil, The Brooklyn Museum,
Gift of Mrs. C. H. De Silver in memory of her husband

*M*ost painters who returned to America after studying abroad settled in New York, which had become the art center of the country. The New York studio of William Merritt Chase, one of The Ten, was a popular meeting place for students and fellow painters. The painting above captures a moment as a woman turns a page of a large album in Chase's cluttered studio.

This view of New York's Union Square in the late afternoon on a wintry day is by Childe Hassam, another of The Ten. The snow casts a veil over the entire picture, blurring outlines and softening shapes. Blurred outlines made with short brush strokes are typical of impressionist paintings.

1890, oil, The Metropolitan Museum of Art,
Gift of Miss Ethelyn McKinney, 1943,
in memory of her brother, Glenn Ford McKinney

1881, oil, The Metropolitan Museum of Art, Purchase, 1895

*S*hortly after the Civil War, the Metropolitan Museum of Art was formed in New York, which had become the third largest city in the world. Its first exhibition of paintings was held in an old dancing school. By 1872 the museum had moved into its own temporary quarters. In the view above by Frank Waller, a visitor to the museum is enjoying an exhibition.

In 1869, the year in which the Metropolitan Museum was organized, the tracks of the Central Pacific Railroad were connected with the Union Pacific Railroad at Promontory Point, Utah. A golden spike was driven into the connecting rails, signifying the linking of East and West. Some railroad stations across the country looked like this one, painted by Edward Lamson Henry. Horse-drawn carriages took people to and from the depots before the automobile was invented. The scene is busy with activity as men, women and children hurry to the waiting train.

The 9:45 Accommodation, Stratford, Connecticut, 1867, oil,
The Metropolitan Museum of Art, Bequest of Moses Tanenbaum, 1937

Grand Canyon of the Yellowstone, by Thomas Moran, 1872, oil,
U.S. Department of the Interior, National Park Service

Rock at Glacier Point, Yosemite,
by William Henry Jackson, about
1885, Denver Public Library
Western Collection

*I*n 1872 America's first National Park, Yellowstone,
was established. At that time, very few Easterners
had ever gone West. Thomas Moran, a painter, and
William Henry Jackson, a photographer, were mem-
bers of a government surveying team that explored
in the West. Moran's paintings and Jackson's
photographs helped convince the United States Congress that the natural beauties of the Yellowstone
region should be preserved.

The Terminal, 1893, Georgia O'Keeffe for the Estate of Alfred Stieglitz

*I*n its early days, photography was a cumbersome process. Immediately before each exposure, a light-sensitive glass plate had to be prepared in a totally dark area. In the 1880's George Eastman found a way to use flexible celluloid instead of glass plates to make photographic negatives. Celluloid could be wound into rolls, which made picture-taking cheaper and easier.

Alfred Stieglitz was interested in recording a simple human event at a fleeting moment. He would wait for hours to take a photograph at just the right time. Above, a horse-drawn car has come to a stop amid the trampled snow at the end of the trolley line. Steam rises from the animals' bodies into the cold air.

While a few industrialists and businessmen were amassing great wealth, most people in America were less fortunate. Many worked long hours in sweatshops for very low wages. Jacob A. Riis, a Danish immigrant who had become a newspaper reporter in New York, used his camera to record the slum conditions in which many immigrants lived, as shown below.

Mullen's Alley (detail), 1888, Museum of the City of New York, The Jacob A. Riis Collection

$\mathscr{W}$ith the development of photography, extremely rapid exposures, as fast as 1/500th of a second, could be made. To study the human body in action, the painter Thomas Eakins used a camera to take pictures of athletes running, jumping, walking, swinging weights and throwing balls. He took these photographs

of a pole-vaulter as a series of fast exposures which registered a sequence of action on a single negative. The new art of photography was opening up new ways of seeing the world for painters.

Eakins painted scenes of boating, wrestling, swimming and other sports. He was so interested in mastering the form and movement of the human figure that he attended classes in anatomy at a medical school. In *Baseball Players Practicing,* he showed the muscles in the players' arms as they wait for the pitch.

Max Schmitt in a Single Scull, 1871, oil, The Metropolitan Museum of Art,
Alfred N. Punnett Fund and Gift of George D. Pratt, 1934

Eakins, who lived in Philadelphia, often went boating with a champion
oarsman. In the river scene above, he has turned around to look at us; behind
him, to the right, is the artist himself. Eakins not only made drawings to help
decide where to place each object in his paintings, but also built little models
of figures and boats to get the proportions right and to create the appearance
of real life. He is known as a "realist" painter.

$\mathcal{F}$rederic Remington was one of the first artists to show horses in motion accurately. He studied photographs of running horses, taken in rapid sequence, to observe the actions of the animals' legs. Remington went West to paint cowboys, Indians and cavalrymen. This painting records a cavalry maneuver: the men rode into battle four abreast, and three dismounted to fight while the fourth led the horses away.

Dismounted: The Fourth Troopers Moving the Led Horses, 1890, oil, Sterling and Francine Clark Art Institute, Williamstown, Massachusetts

$\mathcal{A}$ little boy playing soldier is the subject of this painting by William Harnett. The boy put on a hat made from a folded newspaper, picked up a broomstick to serve as a gun and stood at attention, his back against a wooden fence. Harnett painted every detail, including the print on the newspaper page and the wrinkles in the paper hat, the unmatched buttons on the boy's vest, and the letters carved into the wooden fence and printed on the tattered posters.

Harnett liked to "fool the eye." He copied objects so carefully that the viewer

1888, oil, The Metropolitan Museum of Art, Catharine Lorillard Wolfe Fund, 1963

thinks he is looking at the real thing, instead of a painting. In *Music and Good Luck* a fiddle and bow, a piccolo on a string, a horseshoe and a sheet of music of an Irish song hang from a cupboard door, as though ready to be used at any moment. Also hanging are a box of matches, a calling card with the artist's signature and an open lock. The careful painting of the shadows behind the objects adds to their reality.

Attention, Company!, 1878,
oil, Amon Carter Museum,
Fort Worth, Texas

*T*he one hundredth anniversary of the signing of the Declaration of Independence in 1776 was celebrated with a World's Fair, held in Philadelphia. At the 1876 Centennial, there were industrial exhibits where visitors could see new machines and inventions, such as a powerful steam power generator, a telephone and a typewriter. A picture of Memorial Hall, where the arts were exhibited, was woven into a woolen coverlet made on a machine-powered loom. Until machine weaving was introduced exactly fifty years before the Centennial, all cloth in America was woven by hand.

The World's Columbian Exposition, held in Chicago in 1893, brought together products from all the industrialized countries in the world. Buildings imitating marble temples of ancient Greece and Rome were erected on grounds landscaped by Frederick Law Olmsted. A huge statue representing the Republic was designed by Daniel Chester French, and the great Columbia fountain by Frederick William MacMonnies. Visitors could arrive by rail or boat and view the magnificent fairgrounds from walkways, gondolas or even from the top of a huge Ferris wheel. At night a giant steam engine turned a dynamo that generated electricity so that the grounds were bathed in light.

Photograph by C. D. Arnold, courtesy of Professor George B. Tatum

For the Columbian exposition, the architect Louis Sullivan designed the Transportation Building in which the newest Pullman sleeping cars and railroad locomotives were on display. Sullivan was a pioneer in designing multi-story buildings in America. High-rise structures became possible when the use of metal beams and columns was developed, when electric power became available, the elevator and the telephone were invented and modern plumbing and central heating came into use.

Chicago, Illinois, is considered the birthplace of the skyscraper. The Auditorium Building in Chicago, left, was designed by Sullivan and a co-worker, Dankmar Adler, who solved the difficult engineering problems. It contained four hundred rooms for guests, one hundred and thirty-six offices, and a dining room on the tenth floor with a view of Lake Michigan. The building also included a theater, which was the first ever to be air conditioned; the air was cooled by sprays of water on the roof.

1887–1889,
courtesy of Avery Library,
Columbia University

Built 1869–1883, lithograph by
Currier and Ives 1874, Library of Congress

Steel, for a long time a rare and costly material, became generally available after a process for manufacturing it inexpensively was perfected. Great engineering feats using steel became possible. One of the most daring achievements was the building of a suspension bridge, then the largest in the world—the Brooklyn Bridge. It spans the East River in New York City, connecting Manhattan and Brooklyn. The roadbed is suspended from four cables of steel wires hung from two towers. The pointed arches were designed after European Gothic cathedrals. A walkway above the traffic gives strollers a view of New York harbor. John Roebling, an engineer, designed the bridge. When he died, his son, Washington Roebling, took over the responsibilities for completing the span.

1877, oil, The Metropolitan Museum of Art, Gift of Lyman G. Bloomingdale, 1901

The late nineteenth century was a time of great industrial growth in America. More and more people moved from farms to cities to work in factories, and boat-loads of immigrants poured into American ports to swell the ranks of the workers.

In the scene above, workmen in a foundry are forging a shaft for a side-wheel steamboat. The glow from the furnace and from the white-hot metal casts light on the straining men. The painting is by John Ferguson Weir, whose father, Robert Weir, and brother, Julian Alden Weir, were also well-known artists.

Workers in a steel mill are relaxing on their noon hour in the realist painting below by Thomas Pollock Anshutz. The painter used photographs to study the muscular structure of the human body, which he showed in a great variety of poses. Anshutz, who studied under Eakins, became an important art teacher in Philadelphia.

Ironworkers Noontime, about 1882, oil,
Collection of Mr. and Mrs. Howard N. Garfinkle

1876, oil, The Cooper-Hewitt Museum of
Decorative Arts and Design, Smithsonian Institution

*W*inslow Homer, known for his magazine sketches of Lincoln's inauguration

and the Civil War, was one of America's greatest realist painters. He loved

nature and spent many summers hunting, fishing and sketching in the

mountains. Homer painted both the joys and perils of the outdoors. Barefoot

country children in the midst of everyday activities were favorite subjects,

as shown by these boys in a field eating watermelon.

Homer was interested in the power and loneliness of the sea. For the last twenty-five years of his life, he lived alone on the Atlantic coast in Maine. On a visit to the West Indies, he made watercolor studies for a painting of a shipwrecked sailor after a hurricane. The unfortunate man lies on the deck of a damaged boat, while sharks swarm around the helpless craft. A ship can be seen in the distance. We wonder what the fate of the sailor will be.

The Gulf Stream, 1899, oil, The Metropolitan Museum of Art, Catharine Lorillard Wolfe Fund, 1906

Toilers of the Sea, before 1884, oil on wood, The Metropolitan
Museum of Art, George A. Hearn Fund, 1915

Albert Pinkham Ryder, born in New Bedford, a seaport in Massachusetts, never lost his

fascination with the mystery of the sea. Even after he moved to New York City, Ryder painted

dreamlike, moonlit seascapes of sailboats on moving waters. Often working with a palette

knife instead of a brush, he would add layer upon layer of paint to his pictures, sometimes

over a period of many years. There are no details in Ryder's paintings, only large, solid shapes.

$\mathcal{M}$artin Johnson Heade painted every possible detail in his studies of birds and flowers. From childhood Heade had an interest in hummingbirds and traveled as far as South America to study them in their natural environment. He wrote about hummingbirds and painted many pictures of them. The bird at rest on a branch, right, is smaller than the tropical flowers that surround it.

Hummingbird and Passion Flowers, about 1875–1885, oil, The Metropolitan Museum of Art, Gift of Albert Weatherby, 1946

Third quarter of nineteenth century, oil on composition board,
Abby Aldrich Rockefeller Folk Art Collection, Williamsburg, Virginia

𝒫eople of all ages enjoying themselves at a quilting party is the subject of this

painting by a self-taught artist, who did not sign his work. The picture was copied

from a magazine illustration. Quilt-making was popular during the nineteenth

century. To make pieced quilts, thousands of pieces of cloth were cut into shapes

and sewn side by side into a large overall design for the top of the quilt. A

Pieced quilt, last quarter of nineteenth century, The Brooklyn Museum

backing of the same size was tacked to a quilting frame, and a soft filler, such as cotton or feathers, was spread over it. Then the top was stitched to the back.

When a girl was preparing for her wedding, her neighbors and friends would gather to help stitch her quilt. In the evening, men would join the ladies at the quilting bee for refreshments and dancing.

*E*astman Johnson painted people as he observed them engaged in their daily activities. Whether farmers at work or well-to-do people in their town houses, Johnson painted his subjects with warmth and sympathy.

One day he watched a group of children playing about an old stage-coach. They had thrown their school books aside and were pretending to be horses, drivers and passengers, while two more children came to join the fun.

Johnson was one of America's most important genre painters. Pictures that tell stories of everyday life are called genre paintings.

The Old Stagecoach, 1871, oil, Layton Art Gallery Collection, Milwaukee Art Center

*M*illionaires of the Gilded Age lived in enormous houses modeled after Renaissance chateaux in France and palaces in Italy. The Breakers was the summer home of Cornelius Vanderbilt II. The seventy-seven-room house, constructed of Indiana limestone, stands in Newport, Rhode Island, on a cliff overlooking the Atlantic Ocean. Richard Morris Hunt, the architect who designed it, had studied at an art school in Paris, the

École des Beaux-Arts, and had designed the base for the Statue of Liberty. Sculpture was a very important part of the decoration in a building of this period. Hunt worked closely with the sculptor Karl Bitter, who carved ornaments, a fireplace and a fountain for the house.

The entrance hall of The Breakers is two stories high, like the great halls of European castles in the Middle Ages. Balls and receptions were held here. The walls are faced with stone from France and ornamented with Italian and African marble. The Breakers was built at a time when electricity was not yet reliable, so the chandeliers and lamps are piped for gas as well as wired for electricity.

1892–1895, The Preservation Society of Newport County

*W*hen railroads made travel comfortable, large resort hotels became popular. The Hotel del Coronado in California, designed by James and Merritt Reid, is a rambling wooden structure built around an open patio, following a Spanish tradition. The architecture is a mixture of styles. The timbered, peaked turrets are based on the English Renaissance style known as "Queen Anne." The Del Coronado was the first hotel in the world to use electric lighting. This photograph was taken several years after it had been built and following the invention of the automobile.

As cities became crowded, apartment houses were built to make fuller use of the land. The Dakota, one of the earliest multi-dwelling structures in New York, had huge apartments equipped with electricity, plumbing and central heating. It was designed by Henry Janeway Hardenbergh in the German Renaissance manner, with peaked roofs and carved ornaments. The Dakota is across the street from Central Park, 840 acres of greenery to be enjoyed by the people in New York City. Frederick Law Olmsted and Calvert Vaux were the landscape architects who designed the park.

Dakota 1880–1884, Central Park completed 1876, photograph by
Percy Byron 1894, Museum of the City of New York, The Byron Collection

It was a fashion of the late nineteenth century to set stained-glass windows in new houses. John La Farge, who designed this window, studied art in Paris and brought back to America the idea of using window designs taken from Gothic cathedrals. Stained-glass windows are made from panes of colored glass, separated by strips of lead that form a pattern.

Louis Comfort Tiffany was the leading glassmaker of the period. Through chemical experiments, he developed a technique for fusing together melted glass of various colors and then blowing the molten mass into graceful shapes. He patented his method of glassmaking, by which he

1878–1879, The Metropolitan Museum of Art, Gift of Susan Dwight Bliss, 1930

made what he called "Favrile Glass," and set
up the Tiffany Glass and Decorating
Company, an organization of designers,
craftsmen and decorators.

In Paris, Tiffany glass was sold at
a shop called Maison de l'Art Nouveau.
The term "art nouveau" was given to
a new European art style that turned
away from old designs. Objects in the
art nouveau style have long, flowing,
twisting lines and are often in the shapes
of flowers, leaves or waves. Tiffany was
one of the few Americans whose works
became known internationally as examples of
art nouveau. At right are a vase decorated
with a peacock feather design and a stemmed
vase in the shape of a flower. Both are made
of Tiffany's Favrile Glass.

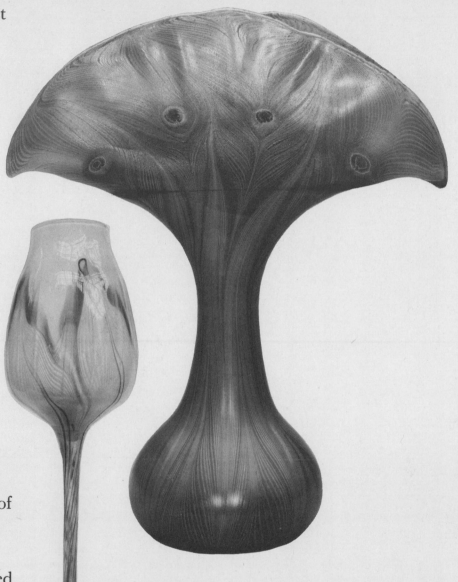

About 1892–1896,
The Metropolitan Museum of Art,
Gift of H. O. Havemeyer, 1896

1895, pen and ink, The Metropolitan Museum of Art, Gift of
Fern Bradley Dufner, The Will Bradley Collection, 1952

This drawing, with flowing, curving lines, is another example of the art nouveau style. It is an illustration by Will H. Bradley, a book designer who was also a poster artist, printer, writer, furniture designer and publisher.

The illustration is from a book of short stories called *Fringilla*. One of the stories is about an artist, Pausias, who meets a young woman, Glycera, gathering flowers in the forest. In this scene, the artist is preparing to paint the lovely lady surrounded by flowers. Pausias paints Glycera and the flowers so skillfully that the picture is as beautiful as nature. Then he sadly learns that Glycera must return to the gods.

The swirling lines in the framing

of the pen and ink drawing, right, show the influence of art nouveau. The picture is from *The Merry Adventures of Robin Hood,* by Howard Pyle, who wrote and illustrated a series of children's books about the Middle Ages.

In this episode, Robin Hood is with his men in Sherwood Forest when a young man dressed in scarlet walks by slowly, sniffing a rose. Robin challenges the stranger to a duel, but the newcomer turns out to be his cousin. Because of his brightly colored clothes, Robin Hood names him Will Scarlet.

Pyle would study the history and costumes of a period so that the setting of his books would be correct and the characters seem real.

Merry·Robin·ſtops·a·Stranger· in·Scarlet :·

1883

The Minute Man, by Daniel Chester French, represents a militiaman of the Revolutionary War, which was fought one hundred years before the statue was made. A young man has dropped his plow and picked up his musket to fight for independence.

The sculptor grew up in Concord, Massachusetts, where the statue stands. Before making *The Minute Man,* French studied a copy of an ancient figure of Apollo. He started with sketches and then made a small clay model. Next, the full-size version was modeled in clay on a metal armature, or frame. From this an exact plaster figure was made, which was sent to a foundry to be cast in bronze, the principal material used for statues in this period. Because bronze statues are first modeled in clay, the sculptor could make figures in dramatic poses with richly textured surfaces.

1897–1903, photograph by Bob Zucker

A statue of the Civil War hero, General William Tecumseh Sherman, stands in New York City. Sherman posed eighteen times while the sculptor, Augustus Saint-Gaudens, made a bust, a portrait of the general's head and chest. The bust served as a model for this large figure of Sherman on horseback, being led by Victory.

1898, The Metropolitan Museum of Art,
Rogers Fund, 1919

The Sun Vow, by Hermon Atkins MacNeil, was said to have been inspired by a Sioux Indian initiation ceremony in which young boys of the tribe had to prove their skill with a bow and arrow.

Like almost all American sculptors of the Gilded Age, MacNeil studied in Paris at the École des Beaux-Arts.

The nineteenth century closed quietly. The United States, no longer primarily an agricultural nation, had become one of the great manufacturing powers of the world, with its industry constantly expanding. Gigantic factories were being built, employing millions of people. Confident of the country's power and proud of its wealth, Americans were ready to move forward with great energy into the twentieth century.